Out of Silence

Out of Silence

Poems by Pamela Harrison

David Robert Books

© 2009 by Pamela Harrison

Published by David Robert Books
P.O. Box 541106
Cincinnati, OH 45254-1106

Typeset in Garamond by WordTech Communications LLC,
Cincinnati, OH

ISBN: 9781934999608
LCCN: 2009929123

Poetry Editor: Kevin Walzer
Business Editor: Lori Jareo

Visit us on the web at www.davidrobertbooks.com

Acknowledgments

I am grateful to the editors of the following magazines in which some of these poems first appeared, in somewhat different form:

Blues for Bill: A Tribute to William Matthews: "Magic Lantern"
Calliope: "Where the Ripples Start" (as "Piano Lesson")
The Contemporary Review: "Aquamarine"
The Georgia Review: "Winter's Tale"
Green Mountains Review: "Triangle of Light"
Pastoral: "Thaw"
Prolog: "Elegiac Heart"
Xanadu: "Dreamhouse, with Lion"

"Triangle of Light" was reprinted in *The College Handbook of Creative Writing* by Robert DeMaria, Harcourt Brace Jovanovich, New York, 1991, and in *Stereopticon*, David Robert Books, Cincinnati, 2004.

My thanks to the MacDowell Colony and the Vermont Studio Center for fellowships during which some of these poems were begun. I am indebted to Barbara Dimmick, Gary Lenhart, Cleopatra Mathis, and Dennis McCullough for their invaluable help toward shaping the final version of this book; to Ann Moore, Nancy Perkins, Suzanne Rhodenbaugh, Carl Rosenstock, and Carol Westberg for their insightful early readings of the poems; to Heather Bagley, Sue Burton, Anne Shivas, and Clyde Watson for their lively and challenging literary companionship; and to Stephany Clothier, Kate Newby, Lynn Harrison, Jr., and my husband, first and always, for their unfailing love and support.

For my brother and sister

What parents leave you
is their lives

—Frank Bidart, "Lament for the Makers"

Contents

I. Truth to Tell

The telling is the madness expelled
—David Denby

Her Wisteria

Beside our house, visible from the table
Mother set for all our breakfasts,
stood a stone fountain whose barefoot girl

waited to fill her urn within the shelter
of an over-growing vine—wisteria's
gnarled wood my father pruned each March

to spur the growth of pendant flowers and make
a fragrant bower for my mother. Lavender
haloed the maiden's head as she leaned dreaming,

chin upon her hand, and the over-flowing water fell
into a scalloped pool where songbirds flew
to slake their thirst all summer long.

March again,
and the empty unsprung fields are raked
by winds that slick the roads.

March, the month of Mother's birth,
on the very day the earth's vernal scale
comes briefly to rest, balancing

the shortened night with lengthened day. In this pause,
when the land lies in its breathless trance,
the starving spirit longs for the season's turn.

Artesian

When you are a child, every day plays
like a stream over a bed of pebbles.
All you can see is liquid and light,
        your future a dream of hazy waiting.

In time, you travel back along a cut bank,
past trees whose runneled trunks stand
like sculpted pillars of a vault.
        High crowns darken the gloom.

At each step, dust motes lift in shafts of ambered light,
hushing your approach to the muscular rush
that fountains up: countless icy gallons
        welling from the world's hidden heart.

Aquamarine

That summer, I spent every waking hour
at a swimming pool sunk in the red dirt
east of town. Mother dropped me there.
I don't know how she passed her days.

It was the year her picture changed.
Her smile was darkly lipsticked on,
her eyebrows painted to a point as though
she was caught in some permanent surprise.

Now she's gone, what I recollect
is being in the water alone, bobbing
in the deep end, rising on a downward
stroke of arms, taking a breath and letting it out

all the way to the bottom. I did this for hours,
hearing the laughter and shouts of others,
blowing them away.

Little Curls of Steam

Water trickled softly from her wash cloth,
and little curls of steam clouded the mirror.
I perched after school on the toilet's closed top,
and we talked in the warm tiled room.

Mother bathed with practiced care,
pushing back the cuticle on each finger and toe,
freeing the pale moons risen there.
Her head bent to the work like prayer.

After all these years—still, the sound of water falling,
fragrance of Ivory soap, the unembarrassed grooming
of a woman who never flinched in her nakedness,
who lived in her deepest heart, sequestered.

Little Boy Blue

By the age of three she parsed
the newspaper on her father's lap.
She started second grade at the age of five,
and the teacher picked her to star as Fauntleroy.
Little Vera memorized the script entire.

Don't you wonder what that middle child
of the farmer's scrambling seven thought
when Miss Whateverhernamewas invited
the prodigy home for special fittings
of the aristocrat's satin pants?

Horsehair sofa, starched antimacassars,
and romantic porcelain figurines posed
in the spinster's parlor. Vera must have thought
she'd won a ticket to the World Museum.
Who can say what dreams took hold

as the six-year-old looked down
at her dear teacher kneeling to pin the hem
of knickers radiant as a sapphire sky? Miracles
must have seemed as sure as summer rain.
Mother wouldn't say, whenever she told the story, why

the family had to move so suddenly away,
two days before the show.
Afterwards, she started over as a boy,
wearing her brothers' pants,
insisting she was "Jimmy".

Beauty

Let's say the year was 1928,
when the rains still came, and the plowing of the prairie
and making first money were well under way.
There was hope in the air,
a surety that a man's hard work and perseverance
would overcome past failures, and there
would be no more talk of not belonging.

Imagine ten-year-old Vera Alice,
coming upon the black baby
laid in a basket outside the store,
his new mother waiting
for the room to clear of other customers
before she might enter
and buy her goods.

Sun boiled behind them,
so white in the tall noon
everything under it paled and stalled;
tied mules hung their heads,
sliced at the neck by the hard line
of shadow pitched from the roof.
Nothing moved, nothing except

the nervous mother, slender
and dressed in her Sunday best,
her dark eyes skittering, alert
against any trespass
she might make. Her baby's sleeping face, framed
by the ruffles of his snowy cap
and the starched pleats of his gown

shone like cool confection
in the oasis of shade—
            as close to a thing of beauty
                        to be found in that town.
Wouldn't you want to share him?
            Wouldn't a girl, who hadn't yet
                        learned the hard

            demarcations of class and race,
want to show her own mother
            what she'd discovered
                        like a pot of gold?
And she did—with presumption
            only innocence could pull—she
                        picked that baby up

            and carried him home,
his frightened mother whimpering
            two steps behind, afraid
                        to stay her,
afraid to speak, waving her hand
            as the white child clasped
                        his breathing perfection,

            crossed the back street
to her own home, and on that porch
            called like royalty
                        at the screen door
for her mother to come
            from her churning and see
                        the rare gift life bestowed.

            Imagine now the bewilderment and shame
that bruised the young girl's neck and cheek

when her mild mother rebuked her
shooing her from the door,
refusing to let them in, turning her back
on the offering with a curt
"Take it back where it belongs."

Their Story

The Banker's Son

A banker's youngest son, Lynn
was fond of telling how his father sent him
    off to college with a blank checkbook,
        saying, *Just don't be a damn fool.*

Buzzing around Denver in Stutz Bearcats
with his rich friends, he lived high and wide for a year
    before the banks of Manhattan and Chicago
        started going under.

Soon, Roosevelt's adjustors decided
to scrap the small land banks to keep pin-striped
    brokers in bowler hats from leaping
        off skyscraper ledges.

Seasons too soon, farmers' loans were called.
Crushed against tellers' cages, housewives
    stuffed savings into bulging black purses
        as panicked crowds pushed to get inside.

Paying the town's accounts from his own worth,
Guy Harrison shouldered his neighbors' ruin, watched
    his gold-leafed name scraped from the door,
        then limped away

with two dollars in his pocket.
It wasn't hours before his heart attack. Called home

to work while his father convalesced—
        la-de-da banker's son turned janitor

in the building his father once owned—
Lynn swabbed toilets and spittoons by night,
      nailed roofs and hauled cement by day,
         grateful for any work that paid.

His father's fall reversed the young man's life
and birthed a life-long dream of wealth.
     He chose Oklahoma because
        the whole state smacked of underdog.

His Dance Declined: Hit Parade, 1939

OVER THE RAINBOW: Lynn was too smug, trim and tanned
from his summer job as a park ranger at Mesa Verde *there's a
land that I heard of*, passing around that photo of himself, arms
crossed over his chest in the rolled up sleeves of a brilliant
white shirt *dreams that you dare to dream* wearing khaki jodhpurs
(a word she'd never heard) and polished riding boots, leaning
in that confident way against the stony ruins *where clouds are far
behind*, sporting Navajo silver bracelets, and oh so mum about
those pretty girls.

ALL THE THINGS YOU ARE: He was six years older *I've longed
for adventure*, liked fine things *what did I long for*, was hard-
working, too, paying his rent by running a laundry pick-up
and delivery service at the selvages of the long school day. He
was charming, told good jokes, admired her intelligence *my
heart beats the faster* and thought she was lovely *the promised kiss
of springtime*. He was pretty cute, too.

DAY IN, DAY OUT: She'd been working hard *I needn't tell you how my days begin* earning not much as a surgical nurse *come rain, come shine* for young ride-'em cowboy docs who told off-color jokes loud enough to make her squirm.

DEEP PURPLE: In letters, Vera and Lynn had progressed *in the mist of a memory* to a kind of understanding that led him *breathing my name with a sigh* to expect he'd be her beau *sweet lovers...in my deep purple dreams* at the nurses' September dance.

INDIAN SUMMER: A big band would be playing at the hotel. He was a senior med student now, her favorite. Things could get serious *the ghost of a romance.* Trouble was, *so many dreams that don't come true,* he couldn't dance.

HEAVEN CAN WAIT: Not, anyway, like that skinny junior who had no charm beyond *darlin it's true* his utter mastery *heavenly in your arms* of every jitterbug, fox trot, and waltz a pretty nurse could hope for in one slim night *this is paradise.*

STAIRWAY TO THE STARS: Sitting out that party *where the blue begins* with all those lesser girls *can't we sail away,* watching Vera turn and dip in that weasel's arms drove Lynn very shortly to a proposal *sound of violins* and *high on the crest of a thrill* his most earnest profession of need.

The Whole Wide World

Over the long three days and nights of her train ride,
    sitting up and sleeping beside the window,
        Vera didn't think in words—

old betrayers, so chockablock in her throat
    she could never say what she felt.
        She didn't think in words.

 Drawn along in the rising wind of her hopes,
    she was stirred by the train's swaying motion,
        its mysterious couplings and uncouplings,
lurches and pauses, heavy breathing
    in dark stations where shadowy figures crossed,
        acting in a mystery of their own.

Her way leaned toward him like language winding
    out of silence in a sensuous line of sound, a song
        to fill the yet-unbounded space of their life together,
and all she had to do was sit in the leathered, creaking car,
    carried along within it like the meaning of a dream,
        an intention opening to the world.

Borne on the rails' rhythmic syntax, she was escaping
    the ruined ground of Oklahoma, those vacant plains where
        rags waved from the windows of farmsteads sunk in dust;
crossing deserts over-arched with August's falling stars;
    skirting the Central Valley's broad, blistering fields
        where her own kin had so lately bent at harvest;

gaining the coast and its great bridged city where the blue Pacific
    turned her north and followed after, bowing wave upon wave
        at the feet of majestic trees. All the pinched years
unspooled with the miles behind her, until she arrived
    where, on his half day off, he so impatiently waited,
        and within the hour they married.

But it wasn't weeks before the past reclaimed her—
    her cough a tuberculosis contracted while she'd worked

as ward nurse in the Oklahoma State Sanitarium.
She spent their first year tethered at bed rest within close walls,
watching sunlight edge across the room, and they scraped by
on his intern's twenty dollars a month.

For their first anniversary, he splurged to buy her
a pint of hand-packed vanilla ice cream, which they ate
together in her bed, sharing the spoon.

Mom Called Him "Zeke"

Cut through with the sawing of seventeen-year cicadas,
the heavy heat of August was Dad's favorite time for mowing.

Sporting cracked leather shoes, paint-spattered pants, faded
baseball cap and holey shirt, he cut the corners square.

A woman with big hair drove slowly down Hillcrest, turned
in the neighbor's drive and drove slowly back, studying

the back, side, and front yards before turning onto Pennington
and pulling in the driveway where Lynn, drenched in sweat,

was bending to fill the gas tank of his orange, grass-matted,
self-propelled Jameson walk-behind mower.

She rolled down the air-conditioned Cadillac's window
and lowered her sunglasses to look him over. When she asked

if he always tended that lawn, he replied, "Yes, ma'am."
When she asked how much he got paid for doing the work,

he allowed he didn't get paid any money, "But the lady of the house
lets me sleep with her from time to time."

There was a pause as the woman shot a look at the house,
rolled her window up without a word, and screeched away.

Father

always said, *You never have to apologize for what you don't say.*
If you can't say something nice, don't say anything at all.
When he played golf, he followed proper rules

for throwing clubs: 1) *straight ahead* so as not to delay play;
2) *nothing side-arm* that might injure your partners; and 3)
one try only to retrieve your driver from a tree.

In our Chevrolet, he chauffeured summer tours to see the USA
at ninety miles an hour; triple dips of ice cream passed for lunch.
We trailed after him through fogs of sawdust in backwoods

furniture factories, stirred the curds and whey of Tillamook cheese,
saluted cavalcades of Hershey kisses, cartons of Salem menthols,
and Wonder Bread's waddable loaves. At General Motors

he drove his own slick-finned monster off the line.
He loved laughing himself awake at some funny dream;
two-pound boxes of Mrs. See's nut chocolates;

our massaging his head while he watched TV; telling
eye-popping medical marvels at meals; and settling us for bed
with his latest yarn of Red Cloud the Wonder Horse.

Before I married, he advised, *If you both think*
you're doing 75% of the work, you've half a chance.
Dear man. I'm going to tell our deepest secret.

Truth to Tell

Waiting for a Word

>Through all the slow yellow twilights
of a summer long ago, we kids played
>"Work-up" across the neighbors' yards,
>>and the big boys smacked boomers
that flew far beyond my gloveless catch.
>Mom played solitaire in her room, waiting
>>for my father to come home.

>Oklahoma City was still a cow town.
Oil wells slanting beneath the capitol
>guzzled up green Eden's black detritus,
>>but our city fathers hadn't budgeted
for building a dome. As I memorized
>state capitals in school, it embarrassed me
>>to have our myth so carelessly uncapped.

>On my last visit back, I hauled away
twenty-three garbage bags of rotten food,
>moldy cookbooks and useless utensils,
>>jars of deadly relish, things I couldn't name,
all stranded in the house when mother died.
>Once, in a silence wide as winter fields,
>>Dad drove me to the hospital

>where she lay, reamed out like a hollow doll
by their last try to cut the cancer out.
>I asked him what really happened that day

she'd tried to die so many years before.
I hoped he'd take the chance to share
their human story, how mother found him
after hours with another.

I felt it wasn't mine to name until he did,
but he would not speak. For miles and miles
he drove, staring down the forsaken road
while I stared at him, waiting for a word.
These fifteen years Dad's house has preserved
the stilled Present of a tomb.
Maybe he reckons it Mother's mausoleum.

He says she's not in her grave.
They bought numbered plots, side by side,
with brass plaques the mowers drive right over.
He visited there every day for months,
but all he heard was dry wind in the grass.

Piano Lesson Day and

what a game!
I pulled at the hand

she'd folded neatly
on her chest. So heavy

it dropped from my grasp
and flopped off the bed

palm up, fingers curled
on nothing, coming

29

so slowly to rest,
I laughed.

I laughed, but
she wouldn't rouse.

*

Dad must have called Mom's sister, Mae, to help.
Standing still against the wall, we three kids
watched from a religious remove the mystery enacted.

First we heard the door slam,
then his sprint up stairs to Mother's side where,
leaning near, he raised her eyelid with his thumb.

Then, as strange as anything, he pressed his thumbnail hard
on the pale moon of her own. Nothing.
Next he drove a long tube down her throat

and switched on a green tank that drummed in the room,
and Mae held the bowl to catch
what it stole back from Mother's stomach.

After that, the two of them shrugged her upright on the bed
and poured black coffee down her throat, and it spilled
out the sides of her mouth, staining her best blue spread.

Then they hauled her useless arms about their necks
and dragged her sagging up and down the room,
and her painted toes combed through the shag.

His Grand Jeté

As he pumped Mother's stomach
and slapped her cheeks,
perhaps our father felt caught,

like Cartier-Bresson's man,
in his "defining moment"—
legs splayed in *grand jeté*

as he leapt
into a vacancy
through which he was fated to fall,

crashing messily back to earth,
breaking through the mirror
of our family's happy myth

and taking us all with him—unless
his skill could freeze the moment
magically in air.

Too shameful to name,
that day's events,
he must have hoped,

might fade in time
into vague unknowing. Into not being.
Into never having been.

Physician, Heal

Young Lynn Henry would be a doctor. Nothing could compete
with Dr. Johnson driving his dray to patients' distant homes. Picture
a blue night, the stab of stars, silent snowy mesas on each side.

Hear the wheels creaking, the horses' hooves dully clopping
on the drifted road, the calm of the doctor's gruff reserve balanced
by the boy's straining to see a spark of lamplight by the creek.

Imagine the child's thrill at entering those other lives,
doing the old man's bidding, laying the sacramental tools
neatly on the cloth. He would re-enact that precision

on a troop carrier in the South Pacific, sewing up Marines
while *kamikazis* dived the anchored ship, and, for years to come,
poring over his anatomy books the night before each operation.

And always he would feel that child's first gift of privilege,
the honor of human intimacy in hard times, the trust
his caring earned.

Imagine then the tangle of his grief,
saving Vera, knowing he was no hero
but the very hurt that drove her desperation.

Reckon the terrible, on-going, inescapable
shame of a doctor who could not heal
his marriage or his wife.

House Call

Dark streets in that part of town,
houses squat on the back of their lots,
a neighborhood empty of any sound.

How was it I was there, in my pajamas,
bundled in a blanket beside him on the seat
as we crept down the street like thieves?

Steering with one hand, he aimed
his spotlight's Cyclops eye, skimming
the blank faces of each front porch, searching

for the number spoken on the phone.
Did we speak?
I don't remember words

just the dark made darker by our headlights,
the prying of the spot,
and green dials on the dashboard

that turned his cheek an eerie hue.
When he found the house, he stopped the car,
fetched his black doctor's bag and locked the doors.

I watched the back of his shadowy form fade
across a treeless yard to an unlit porch.
Long moments of nothing. Then, sudden yellow

crack framing him briefly
before he stepped inside, the door closed,
and absence lapped on every side.

The Sound of Sense

The child, wakened, crept
downstairs to listen to her parents' hissing.

Crouched at the kitchen door,
she could not make out their words,

understood nothing
except the anger, their voices

strangled with passion and fear.
She stayed just long enough

to gather the tone of cold division
then stole away

up the stairs avoiding the creaks
that lurked in the risers

back to her bed
beside her sleeping sister.

There, rigid with excitement and dread, she lay,
guilty of knowing, hoarding the gift.

Turkish Rondo

"I was the only risk I ran"—*Rilke*

Ballasted by Mother and Father opposed
at either end, we took our places
round the table's wobbly boat
and floated on a shoreless sea.

Around us, meaning shifted and ran
like water, and I, a desperate rower,
couldn't play with toys or animate
the blinkless souls of dolls.

So filled with restless worry,
my imagination echoed
with the mysteries of a house
where every practical need was met.

Washed and fed, dressed
and sent to school each day,
I was the ghostly girl
who hid when strangers came.

Squatting alone in a closet, I played
and replayed the little yellow record
of Mozart's "Turkish Rondo," twirling
dervish of my speechless heart.

The Measure of Her Means

How else could Mother wreak her love's revenge?
Greek queens did crueler work: Clytaemnestra
netted Agamemnon in his bath, then stabbed
the water crimson as the rug he'd trod. Medea's wrath
poisoned her rival—golden robes, a wreath of twining fire—
then steeled her heart to knife her own three sons.

And isn't it true that Dad's own mother
righteously removed her children from their culprit father
for six-months' cloistering in a hotel penthouse, directing
the dutiful concierge to send their bills back home?
Her sense of entitlement evened the score.
Granddad could beg forgiveness if he dared.

Mother might have skewered Dad's vanity, outed him
to his patients in the *Daily Oklahoman*, changed all the locks
and pinked the crotches of his fancy suits, convened a jury
of his peers, or hung herself like a bell from the bannister—
tolling in the hall when he came in the door. But Mother
measured her means so sparely. Excising herself

from our lives as neatly as taking an eternal nap,
she knew he'd take the rap, answer the questions asked.
Prim as that, she'd withhold herself from him.
Dead or alive, she wouldn't be his again.
She'd fill the vessel of his life with empty air.
Make his hours chime with nothing there.

The Change

Penned in her reserve—strict
withholding—Mother only watched
while others did and spoke.

She stared like lashless eyes,
a woman who tried too late
to light the furnace of her freezing house.

    *

Pity crept in then
with fear and
we began to condescend.

That little stain,
dropped into the clear
water of the stream,

uncurled
and spread,
tainting everything.

II.   Mother's Lamp

What can be said except that suffering is exact
  —Philip Larkin

Elegiac Heart

Sometimes—in the middle of conversations
about asparagus spears and missed appointments—tears appear,
brimming like spring marshes freshening with light.

These tears are the work of the elegiac heart,
whose view is always over the shoulder,
mourning what is lost.

Who can blame the heart
for having its head on backwards,
for naming too late the joy it lately lived?

Eternity's Peaches

We were sent away. After church one August Sabbath,
  Dad's sister Margaret, mothering me, sat me down
    beneath a tree to study verses. Illustrated with sepia
photographs of Rachel's tomb and Jacob's well, my gold-embossed
  HOLY BIBLE was a "self-pronouncing edition,
    translated out of the original tongues"
and punctuated by a little plastic book mark of the Beatitudes
  (which in nervousness or boredom I chewed at the corners).

Ivy-bordered registers, glossy and as yet blank—where future
  Holy Matrimony, *Births*, *Marriages*, and *Deaths*
    were to document my hardly started life—
enjoyed a place of honor between the Old Testament and the New.
  I hadn't yet read a word. The virgin volume
    was precious to me because
in the framed arabesque of the frontispiece my mother
  had inscribed my name with her own hand.

Afternoon light poured down the dry hill, flooding the yard
  with a weight and warmth as golden as peaches:
    "Heaven's blessing," Margaret said, underlining
the day's lessons with a ruler and red pencil: *Watch therefore*
  for ye know not what hour your Lord doth come.
    She meant to ease my learning of a text so rooted in her life
it might have been her recipe for bread. Stunned by the desecration,
  my secret heart rebelled, refusing all instruction in The Word.

*

Dust-shrouded and spider-webbed, the cellar hoarded shelves
  that warped under the weight of quarts Margaret put up
    against the lean years her Bible warned would come.

Sent down to fetch us sweet cling peaches for dessert, Uncle Lloyd
    stamped and growled, then thumped upstairs.
      With mounting fear I faced the door as Judgment
lunged into view: glasses off, hair askew, pawing the air
    in black bear gloves—it looked to me like Kingdom Come.

Blue, Her Color

Passing the piano where I played, Mother
shifted a stack of ironed clothes
to dust with her palm the spinet's top.

A single swipe, and she was gone—and oh,
her tidy drawers, blue dresses hanging square.
I leaned into the folds and breathed her there.

Nothing was worse than her in-taken breath,
her eyes shut tight on any mess we made.
We had found her atop her blue bedspread.

How odd that was. She had a thing about it.
Never, ever, think of playing there. Former
Okie farm girl with no shoes, Mother

folded the favored cover down each night
and made it up each morning—so smooth
it weighed on their bed like a frozen sea.

Sick Day

White curtains bandage
a morning abandoned to the lonely
boredom of a sweaty bed.

Tonsils, maybe, or the flu
raises the red column
Mother times beneath my tongue.

Pursed lips, then rattled knuckles
shaking it down. Surgical nurse, perched
on the edge of my bed, she peers,

starchly assesses my color. A brisk pat,
and she sets on my lap a tray with lime jello,
paper napkin folded on the bias beneath the spoon.

Her one concession, a pastel striped straw
bent in flat ginger-ale. No games,
no puzzles, no cards, no cuddles. No.

She smiles and shuts the door. On her service,
potential lay-abouts are schooled against hooky,
in fact, completely cured.

The Wide World Just a Rumor

First there was the firmament over all.
Still invisible to herself, the child
in her trance floated like Giotto's angels
in a frame without a ceiling or a floor,
without a shadow in the azure air.

Crouching beneath a new formica desk
with grubby fingers laced behind her neck,
she ducked word of A-bombs and tornadoes.
Micky Mantle won baseball's Triple Crown,
but Russia's Sputnik sliced a scar

across October's darkened sky. When
her urgent hunger for the undisclosed
drove her to open her sister's birthday gift,
she was scolded and stormed from the party
swearing to wear a Stevenson pin.

Thus the One cracked into its Many parts,
and difference settled on her like a pall.
When it fell to her to explain it all,
her small soul, made suddenly visible,
glistened in a caul of helpless shame.

Triangle of Light

Imagine the flooding yellow triangle, how it fell
on the threshold, heavy, tilting like a wave cresting
to break into the shadows where I was stranded,
listening, gulping knowledge like a burning cup.

In the kitchen, Mother was speaking softly
to my brother, and I caught her honeyed tone,
slanting like the August light that warmed
the gate, the path, the sloping field.

Now imagine what a Siamese twin must feel,
the searing fire along her breastbone where the knife
severs her from half she ever was, cleaving
a wholeness she will spend her life searching to complete.

Had you happened upon me then, like a driver coming to rest
behind a car in whose rear window a plastic doll nods, agreeing
to everything, you might have sensed my complicity
as something in me acceded—*no*—affirmed

the fitness of her choice: for, *yes*,
I loved him too, naturally, loved him first and best,
and so the moment passed away....Sometimes
it happens now, crossing a snowy yard

over whose chill expanses evening shadows lean,
or stepping from some dim interior into jarring
refractions of sunlight striking crisscross off of traffic:
a moment I pause to remember something

telling myself I must remember
what was once so present and so clear—

though now, only the weight remains,
tangled in the light, in the gold or blue.

Family Circle

It was the birthday Mom turned forty-three.
Again March froze her Easter flowers, but
Dad reserved a table at the Tower Club,
his favorite spot because it was posh,
there was a band, and Mother loved to dance.

When we were dressed, she called us together,
hugging a black purse bulging with bills she'd saved.
We gathered round like show and tell, amazed
to see her take the stage and hear her state
her gift: money enough for us to take a trip abroad.

Dad stepped in asking *where?* What secret destination?
Then the shape of what she meant came down, collapsing
like a circus tent around its center pole: She wouldn't come.
She'd stay—we'd go. I remember how we sat,
leaning into the hidden sense of all she said.

All the pains we had taken, all the months and years
of trying to be good enough to change the doom
of that earlier day, flared in her refusal.
Shamed by her bribe, Father—all of us—
stumbled weeping from the room.

They Also Serve Who Only Stand and Wait

When she was dying Mother confided,
I wasted a lot of time keeping house.
How the slap of her flats had rattled on the stair!
She sped from chore to chore, making our ship
so trim it tightened like a vise.

Regularly, she straightened the fringe
on the parlor rug with a four-inch Fuller comb,
washed and ironed all our sheets and clothes,
pressed Dad's boxers and striped pajamas,
rose in the dark to prepare our breakfast:

vitamins meted in our spoons,
a maraschino cherry planted in the severed eye
of grapefruits she dissected for our ease—her ministrations
as invisible to us then as any sweating stevedore
heaving cargo from a leaking hold.

The winch, the wheel, the will—on whose shoulders
hours were hauled from white dawns to bloody sunsets—
she was the inner working of each day. Salving
the hurt of how she spent her light, under her breath
she'd recite her favorite sonnet.

All the Long Year

Mockingbird

Though it has stolen the summer's first ripe figs,
Father frees the bird from his net before he leaves for work.
Flown out of reach to a live oak branch, it now withholds
the aria that curled down the air like promise all last spring.

That song beguiled us then, as we walked the garden path,
Mother frail between us in her robe and tennis shoes, counting laps
like proof of some reprieve. Along the way, sapphire iris
mingled with lemon lilies then bowed to Rose of Sharon.

Leaning hard, Mother presses on, limping around the circuit
of the season's shortened days. Once, mockingbird
sang over all, calling down our empty chimney,
changing her tune as we passed.

Feeding Tube

Dad couldn't let Mother go,
couldn't bear to lose her again, and so
because already they'd taken so many organs out,
they inserted a feeding tube
hung on a pole above her bed—life line
no one could say *No more* to. But,
as these things go, the cancer ate her faster, and so,
what had been his choice to save her, saved her
for that longer, crueller dying.

The Curving Path

Looking toward his dotage, Dad bade a mason
lay a curving path one wheelchair wide
around our yard. But
it's Mother, six years younger,

I wheel to view the blowing roses
before the sun can sear their petals
and draw the pearls of autumn dew
like departing souls away.

Now we struggle through each night.
She finds Jesus' face in the wallpaper.
Straining forward from the pillow,
arm outstretched, she reaches for a door

that will not open.
When her moaning starts, I run
to waken Dad.
In his striped pajamas, hair deranged

as though the torment of his dreams
had tossed him in a tempest, he
refuses to increase her dose of morphine—
and then we're yelling.

He's afraid, he says, "afraid
she'll get addicted."
"But, Dad, she won't be addicted.
She'll be dead."

Gingerbread House

Downstairs Christmas sets, granular and sweet,
too many ornaments, too much to eat: it cracks
like brittle. I toss on sour sheets, ill and remembering
last fall, how the southern heat rose and fell
as Mother lay in her bed, delirious and gray.
I watched from the corner chair for days.

I've heard this season's tunes too many days.
Now childhood carols I once thought sweet
suffocate like December's blanketing gray.
Lowered over these northern roofs, cracks
of sunlight fade as quickly as they fall
across my quilt. Sick of remembering,

I want the pretense over, remembering
against my will how many family holidays
mixed with illness, how readily we fell
into our cloying refrains—sickly sweet
routines so sugar-coated they had to crack
beneath the weight of expectation. Gray

as ash, I feel Mother's face rising gray
into my own. Am I remembering
or *becoming* her? Sudden panic cracks
the brittle mask. As cycling years and days
swing round their rutted paths, the bitter-sweet
love and doubt of my allegiance fail

to praise her gentle heart. Oh, what a foul
betrayal living is! Mother, your gray
eyes spoke words you were too discreet
to say, and I am left remembering.

Into your frailty you packed our days'
desertions, bathed in hidden gin the cracks

in our family's lying myth, cracks
that grew to fissures until broken pieces fell
like swords around us. Now your dying days
repay our selfish borrowing. In the gray
of this wasted hour, I'm remembering
what I owe—and all you lost by being sweet.

Last Goodbye

Mother, this is the last kiss I intend
to lay on your thin cheek. I take my leave.
It's hard for me to think how this will end.

For months, it's been my honor to attend
you, night and day. I must go home. Please believe.
Mother, this is not what I intended.

None of us will name it. But I won't pretend.
This is the last kiss of mine you will receive.
It's hard for me to think how this will end.

At such a parting fear and sadness blend.
When you awake, you'll find me gone and grieve.
Mother, this is the last kiss I intend.

They've drawn your long death out without amend,
flogging their sorry hopes. I'm not naive.
It's hard for me to think where this will end.

I refuse to conscience what I can't defend.
I can't stand to watch what I can't relieve.
Mother, dear, here's the last kiss I will spend.
I cannot bear to think how this will end.

What the Wind Is

This is what the wind is
good for, Father said
after the storm, bending
to gather up the dead
and fallen branches in the yard.

Final Trial

What was her lingering
but for him, and his constancy
but for her—unless, even then,
the staying and the waiting
bespoke the ancient conflict?

She stayed to try his love;
he stayed to prove it true.
So many days and months, her life—
waning—strained as it withdrew,
as the lips of a shrinking sea
kiss and kiss a widening shore.

Time stretched their love as thin
as gold hammered into the barest
trace of wedding. At last, the physician
in him knowing what would come, he
left her to their watching son and fled.
Minutes after he shut the door

she drew her final breath. Had she won?
Did he lose? Did they suffer into truth?
Let us say in that closing hour the balance
came at last to rest: his penance exacted;
her proud heart appeased.

Fixity

For a bitter year, Mother
struggled to open that heavy vault. At last,
wasted to bone and paper skin, curled
in the middle of her bed, she sighed,
all sixty-seven pounds of her,
and it gave, it gave.

Tonight, the door is open.
I turn about these rooms, weighing
the heft of treasured things, knowing
what killed Lot's wife: her grief,
the salt in her tears, what of herself
she couldn't leave to live.

My Father's Well

Fifty years ago these prairie plains burned
as they are burning now, and Father paid
to drill a well four hundred pipe feet down

into an ancient aquifer: private wealth
he mined to serve his pride while all around
his neighbors' sorry gardens died.

Through intervening years he never learned
to improve the compacted earth from which
his waterings ran away like restless children.

Instead of carting off bales of fallen leaves
and mounds of twice-mown grass, he might have
built the tilth of his domain, giving back

to the crusted ground the rich decay of living,
composted and transformed,
allowing fragile roots to breathe deep down.

In this year's rainless repeat of old withholding—
refusing the balm that baring the past
might bestow—in triple digit heat,

my father hauls two hundred feet of heavy hose
around his acreage. Eighty-nine, a bad heart,
he wants to die there in his yard, green as Eden.

Climbing Sorrow

There is no charted place
for these divestments
no decorous time
to fasten on the secret
spheres of parents except
to root them out of bed
and down a darkened stair
to set things straight
before a dying fire

And then to see
the long shadow cut
through the years
upsetting the universe
rearranging the sun
the moon and stars
with a question
leveled like a poker
at a father's ashen heart

Bitter as sorrow
shivering in the cold
could you
turn the beggar out
the still-mad king
and watch him limp
through the rutted dark alone

Mother's Lamp

I remember finding her in their bedroom, at the lamp,
chipping the cheap paint off with her thumbnail, nothing harsher
for fear she'd mar the finish.

Gaudy carnival junk, I thought, cheap thing she'd salvaged
from their cramped first home: A shepherd in black breeches
and his gold-plated girl, coarse as pirates beneath a too-big shade.

Taking a chance on loss, she labored to unearth it:
patience took the tawdry, too-bright cheerfulness
down in time to real Dresden blue.

III.   The Saving Clue

And the way up is the way down, the way forward is the way back
—T. S. Eliot

Words Deserted

When the honeymoon was over,
we breakfasted in our single room,
Baltic twilight, murmur of morning voices,
clink of spoons in bowls, raspberries'
ruby bruises smothered in thick cream.

Husband of a month, you biked away each day
to the work that took us there, leaving me
to chart a shapeless solitude. Lost
in a tongue whose consonants cracked like cannon fire,
I botched my shopping at the market,

brought home obscene lengths of sausage
to eat with scant loaves of bread.
Haunting stalls where others laughed and talked,
I stared at wares I could not name.
Clerks looked through me and away.

*

Easier then to live inside my head. Bad luck
the library's single English novel was Plath's:
on a park bench beside boozy *pullopojat*
who slept like bears beneath the bushes,
I fell into the vacuum of *The Bell Jar.*

Before that time, I never dreamed how much
I needed language to sustain my self,
piecing thoughts to one cloth, shaping
the straying present into an ordered past.
When words deserted me,

whole days escaped in air.
Beside myself on lonely walks, I was flotsam
drifting across department stores' glass windows,
shreds of color on the harbor's restless water.
Long afternoons, I wedged myself

in a cleft of granite rocks at Kaivopuisto,
watched housewives bludgeoning winter
from their rugs, dirty water sluicing down
the harbor rocks, flocks of white sails, taut
and tilting out to sea.

*

That rudderless day I rode the bus back,
heard the crowd howl a wounded vagrant off:
blood spilled over the heel of his shoe,
left the glistening print of one sole
limping up the aisle.

By the time you biked home, night seeped in
to fill the well of the courtyard, lapping
black at the rim of our window.
When I came unmoored, the room moved,
heeling hard to port as I peeled potatoes.

The yellow disk of light
wheeled from the lamp, slid
from the table, broke across the floor.
You eased the knife from my hand
as gently and firmly as one might close a door.

Echoes in a Field of Thought

My first memory—Mother's *Don't!*
My flowers! the sight of my white tie shoes on dirt
and sudden clutch of guilt.

What pulls me to a stop today is the little girl
in Vickrey's "Flower Garden." On her hands and knees,
she's been decorating the asphalt with colored chalk.

Absorbed in her play, edging unaware
from a deep well of shadow toward the light,
she's filled all the foreground with stars and flowers

beneath whose airy forms on the road's grey
paving, faint fissures slowly show. Gazing at her,
I'm suddenly seized. As care descends to dread,

I want to call out, *Don't!*
But Vickrey pins me there—between her dream
and all that rushes at her back.

Inner Weather

Listen, someone's tapping,
tapping softly, afraid
to make a noise, sink the nail.

Today, so cold
the bolt on the door
is frosted on the inside.

Can a voice be found
as fitted to its mood
as rime on wood?

One story shared
whose telling stills the awful
gnawing of my heart?

Enter Here

Behold the gate
where the way forward
is the way down
To enter here you must

abandon your name, then home
with the genius of grave birds
whose featherless red heads
and oily black wings disgust you

From the reaches of noon, dive
toward the forest's shrouded floor
There you will find the hidden death
that already swells with offal

Pilgrim, you must fall
through a rotting bridge into depths
of layered dark, and you will
fear this falling as you fear your dying

There will be much halting, no progress
only a handless clock ticking eternal
rounds in a stillness that is
the endless here of where you are

*

With each step, the air
gets heavier, hotter;
torch light darkens
from gold to red.

Your hand slides
along the curving wall
as you descend the stone stair,
spiraling counterclockwise

to the castle's nether keep.
At the bottom looms
the gloomy threshold
where a massive weight

slithers in the dark.
From depths then,
your voice escapes
its own black cave,

reptilian scales
plating your throat, coiling
up and up, until you are
the snake you fear.

Where the Ripples Start

"The stars move still, time runs, the clock will strike
The devil will come..." —Christopher Marlowe

I wonder, did Mother rehearse, washing
in silence, watching water trickle from her cloth?
I always saw her with a prop, the broom,
a dishtowel in the doorway while I practiced after school.

Mondays she drove me all the way cross town
for piano lessons in a house where Miss Lord's
stormy paintings glowered on the walls and two
grand black pianos flared like open caskets.

While I stumbled up and down the keys, Mother waited
beneath a tree whose leaves turned in upon themselves.
Passing the hour with *Reader's Digest,* she memorized
the street down which she stared.

Whose dream it was to have me play I couldn't say.
None of the assigned songs sang anything to me.
I knew the drill: we had to leave our house by four—
Miss Lord refused to let a laggard in. I'd seen her there,

through the locked door, seething in her buttoned chair,
star sapphire flashing on her tapping hand. Unlucky stars
that Mother chose the very day I planned to play
so well I'd charm her to forget the time.

Children's magic to think I had the power to stop
the devil's clock with silver strains of "Für Elise".
Past Four! Alabaster Beethoven sneered from above.
Hell's cold fire lit beneath my feet. I ran upstairs.

Sunlight rebounded from polished glass,
and rows and rows of square white tile glowed like rubies
on the water and the scarlet rippling round and round
Mother's white face floating like an island in a flood—

Or so the would-be poet wrote,
then got the shakes so bad they sent her quaking
up the stairs to soak in a bath she hoped
would wash away the guilt. Where do ripples end

that start in breezes from some sandy shore then move
through waters various and deep and in the moving
magnify until they tower in tidal waves?
Now I bathe in the afternoon, as Mother did,

warm water drawn in a murmurless house,
knees afloat, breasts like whitened reefs below
a shine rippling slick against the cool enamel,
pale waves circling in a box. I read about a woman

sitting in her car, lonely as a candle in the dark, spontaneously
igniting in her clothes. I think about it sometimes, wondering
if obsessing could by concentration make a flame.
Would water put it out?

The Eyes Have It

My daughter has an ear for birdsong.
When she whistles, wild wings flutter indoors,
root among her ribbons, pull at the light cord,
fly at feathered rivals in the mirror. All day, I hear her
music winding through our rooms. The world enters
her delicate bones, and she gives it back in song.

For me, the eyes bank all remembrance,
vision's stoppered reservoir pools a long day's tangents
and remorse, images waiting for words, potent and choked:
Curtains of heat hung from the dusty trees.
He pressed the pale moons of her thumbs.
Her toes dragged through the shag like combs.

Broken Lock

I'd find Mother in the kitchen, staring
at closed cupboards while she smoked.
I tried to guess what she didn't say,
a hieroglyph I studied as if I might decipher

the shadings of her voice, screen of words
that lay like lace over luster below. I got so good,
to this day I vibrate at hooded looks, lidded tones,
conflicts waged in civil conversation, the claw

that lurks below the silver surface of a pool.
That day she tried to kill herself, did she
time the pills, counting on us,
her children, to save her?

She posed like Snow White on her bier,
hands folded on her chest,
slippers paired beside the bed.
It was a slap to wake the dullest heart.

Was it a test of love we almost failed?
What could she think she proved
but our unworthiness? We stood like dwarves
beside her peaceful form.

*

When all was done, one child stood at a window
looking out at what she remembers as rain. No one spoke.
Year after year the child grasped at the unsaid.

Denied a name for what had happened, the secret

girl began to steal words from the air, the face
of pages, the backs of throats, loose words

and mutterings uttered behind closed doors,
all the forbidden sounds they'd sealed so deep
it would take years to break the lock.

The Gift of It

When understanding flew to take love's measure, weighing
its exact equivalence to loss, it bound the child
to the mother, one negation inviting another, gift for gift.

Then even the child could see how shadow gave
each thing its weight, made volume visible, enrapturing
her new eyes with all of earth's pending end.

And the miracle was she did not turn away, did not rebel
or raise her ego's opposing sword. Shouldering the dark,
she discovered an identity. In that ethereal moment,

death sired curiosity and compulsion, whetting an appetite
she hadn't known to save in some shaped sound, some
right word found, each glinting bit of Now.

She began by collecting rocks and shells, tiny
bottles, sun pouring through, shine painting
a pitcher's lip, the wind-skinned lake's rising wave.

Reading in the Dark

This is how a way of life begins—in not knowing
in wanting to know, scratching the unanswered itch,
seeking a phrase to fix

a strand of meaning, the timbre of a voice
that, but for the naming,
would slide away into blank forgetting.

This is the practice
by which a curious child more eye than wit
becomes an archaeologist

assembling the puzzle. Up late
in her pitched tent, its slanting canvas lit
by a smoking lamp, she muses on the broken tokens,

throws her imagination back
to that unrecorded time, reading its music and its light
by their own melody and fire.

No Mean Trick

"The teller sets the crooked message straight"—Aeschylus

A pear's green peel exactly fits its own white flesh.
And we must fit our words to the world—or we are mad.

But how agree? When each of us, mother, father, sister, brother,
saw it all so differently? Where were you? When did they? How did we?

Long ago, before departing, divinities dropped their veils, dazzling
the life of the swineherd whose hovel it was.

Rehearsing Adam's task, I'm speechless as a peasant
through whose undefended fields powerful armies drive at will.

Mastering illusion is no mean trick. It takes time and quiet, gazing
until a burnished surface opens into dim and silted depths.

Then practice for hours the art of naming, searching for the single word
that levers feeling's fragile curve on smooth planks of thought.

Magic Lantern

The chairs were hard.
The room was hot.
A poet of his stature
might have been forgiven
for being brief.

Hopeless and ambitious
lovers of his craft, we
crowded in a crescent
toward the brilliant, unscripted
speech that fell with such aplomb
from his mustachioed mouth.

With flawless timing, he focused
the magic lantern of his mind
on foul shots and jazz riffs,
his reflection so gently trained
on all our failures it seemed
we merely overheard a genius
musing to himself.

Wasn't that the magic of the man—
candor joined with kindness
for everyone but himself?
His shirt, when he was done,
was soaked—the only sign
of what those words had cost.

Dreamhouse, with Lion

The kitchen is warm, old brick and the glow of polished copper.
Sitting on a stool where generations have watched and stirred,
he peers into a burnished pot, finds it brimming.

From across the room, she watches as he sets the commodious,
well-turned bowls. Supper simmers, fragrant lemon and thyme.
He is at last at home.

They have traveled great distances to take their place together.
But part of her has not yet arrived. How strange it feels
to leave him and wander further, searching for her own.

Upstairs and down, so many rooms alike, ample and airy,
all she has to do is throw her coat across a bed
and call it hers. But none is hers, nor answers

her inquiring look until a last, low door she thinks too small to give
on more than back streets where milkmen leave bottles on the step
and vagrants pick through litter in the gutter.

You know the freighted way of dreams, how some places
hold the power to make you fear? Think of a glacier,
its dense insistence, icy blue calm.

Or imagine the lightless weight at the very bottom of the sea
where creatures strange and graceless feel their way toward food.
Now see the room she finds—bare, unbecoming, a cell

where no one ever lived, or could, where gravity dims the light.
She backs away explaining, "I must have melody and measure,"
learning the truth then for herself. That's all it takes

for roof and walls to fly and pillars rise, two stories high.
Bathed in morning's clarified light, she beholds
a broad, open floor unfolding ahead and right, commanding

a view over the trees, tiered roofs and towers of a noble city.
When the first strains of music bell into that vast, domed height,
the lion of the house strides, tousled and yawning from its slumber.

And though she turns toward the kitchen where,
even now, her lover rises to find her, though she turns,
yes, from the lion, for the moment afraid,

she knows that place is hers
and she will preside over the dancing,
over all the dangerous celebrations still to come.

The Light Rises

Day will come. Even after you give up,
surrendering the starless field
to the grave of sleep, morning's light

will rise beyond the hills, fiery red against the black,
insisting: You are a creature of that light—see
already the sun

has gilded the frozen slope, and azure
shadows pool in the delicate tracks
of last night's deer.

Winter's Tale

Until today, I never got the logic
of Shakespeare's chilly comedy, why
Hermione stayed all those years away
while time played out the siege of her love's heart.
Now I'm told my mother made my father pay
nine years of penance, sharing a sterile bed. How did they
bear lying between the sheets, side by side each night
under the cold blanket of the other's breathing?

How disciplined they were
before us, never a cross word,
upholding the mindful gloss of courtesy,
nothing alarming, nothing true,
allowing our ignorant, adolescent lives
to billow out of the confines of that starving house.
Such kindness, utterly adult,
never to halve our hearts by telling tales.

That last bad year, I'd call home from college,
catching her in her alcoholic blur, tongue so thickened,
speech so slurred, I hung up without speaking, never dared
to name the suicide she'd begun to live.
Cold at heart and letting the silence grow,
I abandoned them.
My brother did the work: Dad wept to tell him
how ruined he was, and why.

It was my brother, her beloved, who talked her back,
refusing her further refusals, coaxing her to speak.
Weighing out the grains of weeks and months and years,
while I wrote essays on *The Winter's Tale*,
my brother forged words and lay them one by one

against the locked vault of her grief until, at last, it gave.
Leontes chastened. Perdita found. Hermione restored.
Oh, the truth is always larger than the story told.

I have only my part recounted.
Forgive my need to speak at all.
I am the lost child, found; the lost child, loved,
however lost she felt she was.

Thaw

On a March Monday so mild
      the season's songbirds sing,
she puts on her galoshes and passes down
      on old crusted snow to the hollow.

Leaving the path, the sun-bathed bowl
      of meadow and the noisy road
where trucks and cars rush past,
      she steps into the stand of pines

like the deer that sleep beneath its boughs.
      Standing still in that quiet cover,
awakening to the grove's hidden life,
      she soon hears the invisible stream.

Threading toward it through the thawing,
      slipping, catching a bare branch,
she follows the sound down to a pool
      where silver trickles over ice. There,

she lies down on a bed of fallen needles
      and gazes up though the intricate
etchings of bare limbs toward the green-
      needled height. She thinks

maybe she'll make a little room there
      above the rusted floor, clearing
some space, simplified and chaste.
      For now, it's enough to rest a while

near the whispering, hearing again
      the world's pulse freed from loss.

The Saving Clue

Each spring the pear tree burns in a white cloud of bloom,
and I remember, Mother, the light on your face
as you scanned your thesaurus. Spying your rapt intent,

I envied each syllable you spoke, snapping the old book shut
as though you'd found a saving clue, raising the hope
of words like guiding stars into my night.

How could you burn all your journals? Mother, for years
I've kept the leather-bound gift you thought I never used
because I stored our treasure in its tissued box.

Searching, sounding for depth, I've sat so long at this work,
the weathered case has cracked. This morning, a melting stream
escapes its thatch of winter grass, and I lay these words upon its waters.

Genesis

There is nothing else
you will settle for.

Though there is breaking.
Though the walls fall down.

Though the most precious stones
of the citadel you have built

lie forever in rubble.
You will have nothing

less than the world.
Lit by ghosts of stars,

alone on a herdless plain,
at dawn you will rise

and walk
in any direction.

Notes:

"Her Wisteria"
Reading Aeschylus's *Oresteia,* that greatest of family tragedies, around the time of my mother's birthday, I was inspired by Robert Fagles' explanation of the Greek Anthesteria as a "festival of libations which summoned the spring by summoning the great ancestral dead as the source of all new life...a rite of spring...when the God is struggling for rebirth, when winter yields to March."

"Mom Called Him 'Zeke'"
Grateful thanks to my brother for a full rendering of this incident.

"The Sound of Sense"
The title of this poem refers to that quality of speech with emotional import first articulated by Robert Frost as the source of his special kind of music:

> "I alone of English writers have consciously set myself
> to make music out of what I may call the sound of sense."

"Turkish Rondo"
The epigraph is taken from Rilke's "Requiem on the Death of a Boy".

"They Also Serve Who Only Stand and Wait"
The title is a line from Milton's sonnet, "When I consider".

"Climbing Sorrow"
The title is taken from *King Lear,* Act II, Scene iv, ll. 57.

"Words Deserted"
Pullopojat is Finnish for "Bottle Boys". I am grateful to Liisa
Bradley for the proper spelling of the term.

"No Mean Trick"
The epigraph is taken from Aeschylus's *The Libation Bearers*.

"Magic Lantern"
Written in memory of William Matthews, and first published
in *Blues for Bill: A Tribute to William Matthews,* Kurt Brown, Ed.,
Akron Series in Poetry, University of Akron Press, 2005.

Breinigsville, PA USA
25 September 2010
246079BV00001B/55/P